William Ralph Douthwaite

Gray's Inn

Notes illustrative of its history and antiquities

William Ralph Douthwaite

Gray's Inn
Notes illustrative of its history and antiquities

ISBN/EAN: 9783337282653

Printed in Europe, USA, Canada, Australia, Japan

Cover: Foto ©Andreas Hilbeck / pixelio.de

More available books at **www.hansebooks.com**

GRAY'S INN

NOTES

ILLUSTRATIVE OF ITS

HISTORY AND ANTIQUITIES.

COMPILED BY

W. R. DOUTHWAITE,

LIBRARIAN.

LONDON.
1876.

EARLY HISTORY OF GRAY'S INN.

It has been observed by a modern writer that Holborn has long been famous as a law quarter of London. Gray's Inn, Staple Inn, Barnard's Inn, Furnival's Inn, and Thavie's Inn are all in the neighbourhood of Holborn. Some idea of the neighbourhood in the time of Elizabeth may be obtained by reference to the map of Ralph Agas. Holborn there appears as an open country road, commanding a northward view of the Hampstead and Highgate Hills, and of the little "lonely, almost forsaken, church of St. Pancras" midway. A few houses and shops by Holborn Bars, and the gardens and buildings of Gray's Inn are seen, with Gray's Inn Lane, the houses in which then extended no farther than the Inn. Four of the

B

Gray's Inn Lane houses, looking like houses built of cards, one storey projecting over another, still remain as specimens of the buildings in Elizabeth's time.

Gray's Inn was esteemed a most agreeable resort on account of its retirement, and was frequented not only by barristers and students of the law, but by divines and literary men. Sir Samuel Romilly in a letter to his sister, dated from his Chambers in Gray's Inn Square, in 1780, says, " My rooms are exceedingly lively . . . . the moment the sun peeps out, I am in the country, ... having only one row of houses between me and Highgate and Hampstead."

Among the distinguished literary men who resided here, may be mentioned the illustrious Lord Macaulay, who, between the years 1829 and 1834, occupied chambers at 8, South Square, afterwards taken down for an extension of the Library.

Gray's Inn stands upon the site of a property anciently known as the Manor of Portpoole, or Purpool, and is generally supposed to have derived its name from the noble family of the Greys of Wilton. Domesday Book gives no account of the Manor of Portpool. Holborn, however, is mentioned thus :—" At Holeburne the King has two cottagers, who render yearly twenty pence to the King's Sheriff. The Sheriff of Middlesex always had charge of these cottagers in the time of King Edward. William the Chamberlain renders yearly to the King's Sheriff six shillings for the land where his Vineyard is set."

A very large portion of the Hundred of Ossulston, in which Gray's Inn is situated, appears to have belonged to the Bishop and Canons of St. Paul; and from the Manor of Portpool, an ancient prebend of St. Paul's Cathedral takes the name. In the list of prebendaries of St. Paul's Cathedral, given in Dugdale, the name of Theobald stands as the first prebendary of Port-pool; no date is given of his collation, but he is supposed to be the same person who occurs as Archdeacon of Essex in 1218, and again in 1228.

According to Archdeacon Hale, the records of the Cathedral of St. Paul's exhibit no conclusive evidence when, or under what circumstances, either the Chapter as a body, or the prebendaries as individuals, became possessed of their lands and manors; and Portpool seems to have been one of those portions of the Cathedral property which formed the separate estate of one of the Canons.[a]

Portpool is also mentioned in the reign of Henry III.

---

[a] Domesday of St. Paul's, introd., p. iv.

In the Fine Rolls, 42 Henry III. (1258), it is stated that, " William le Bacheler and Isabella his wife give half a mark for one assize of novel disseisin, taken before the Justices at Westminster, against Simeon de Gardio and others of tenements *in the ways of Holeburn and Purtpol, in the suburb of London.*"[a] And in Parton's Account of the Parish of St. Giles in the Fields, it is stated that one, "*Robert de Purtepole,*" by Deed dated 46 Henry III. (1262), gave to the Hospital of St. Giles (*int. al.*), ten shillings annual rent, issuing from his house, St. Andrew Parish, to find a Chaplain to celebrate his anniversary obit in the Hospital Church.

The earliest mention hitherto found of the *Manor* of Portpool, is in the 22 Edward I. (1294), when the Dean and Chapter of St. Paul's Cathedral were summoned to appear before the Justices itinerant, to answer by what warrant they claimed to have a Court Leet and various other liberties in Chiswick, Sutton, and other places, and in *Purtepol Sokne.* The following is an extract from the Quo Warranto Rolls :—

" The Dean and Chapter of the Church of St. Paul were summoned to answer the Lord the King of a Plea by what warrant they claim to have view of frankpledge

---

[a] " Excerpta é Rotulis Finium," vol. 2, p. 265.

and the amends of breach of the assize of bread and
ale, pillory, tumbrel, infangethef, outfangethef, gallows,
chattels of fugitives, condemned persons their tenants,
year and waste of their lands, and the amerciaments of
their men in, among other places, *Purtepol Sokne* and
Fynesbury Sokne. And the Dean and Chapter they
come, and the Dean saith that he found the aforesaid
Church seized of the aforesaid liberties, and that he ought
not to answer thereupon, without the Bishop of London.
And the Bishop is present, and freely joins himself with
the aforesaid Dean and Chapter in answering, who say,
that they and their predecessors *from time whereof memory*
is not, have had all the Liberties aforesaid in the aforesaid Vills, and have used the same without interruption, and except that they have not had Gallows
otherwise than in Fynesbury Sokne, at which they   .
have caused Judgments to be executed on the condemned of their Tenants of all the Vills aforesaid,
and this from the aforesaid time when memory is
not, and by this warrant they claim the Liberties
aforesaid."

    The Jury elected for this purpose say upon their
oath " that the aforesaid Bishop, Dean and Chapter *have*
had the aforesaid Liberties in their aforesaid Manors, and
have freely used them from time whereof memory is

not, without any interruption. Except that they have not had nor have they Gallows otherwise than in the aforesaid Vill of Fynesbury, and they say that when any man of their aforesaid Vills hath been taken, they cause to assemble 20 men each having his two hides of lands to proceed to Judgment upon him.

" Therefore the aforesaid Bishop, Dean and Chapter go without a day saving the right of our Lord the King," &c.[a]

These proceedings in Quo Warranto, clearly show that the Manor of Portpool belonged in ancient times to the Dean and Chapter of St. Paul, London.

---

[a] " Placita de Quo Warranto," 22 Ed. I.

THE DE GREY FAMILY, THEIR CONNECTION WITH THE PROPERTY, AND THE ACQUISITION OF IT BY THE SOCIETY.

ACCORDING to Dugdale, the family of the De Greys was descended from Henry de Grey of Codnar. The exact time when the Manor of Portpool came into their possession has not been ascertained.

Reginald de Grey, the first of the family mentioned in connection with the property, died in the first year of Edward II. (1308). An Inquisition, taken after his death at " *Purtpole*," states, that he died seized of a messuage and certain lands there, and of rents of assize, which he held of the Dean and Chapter of St. Paul, London, by rent, service, and suit, at their Court Baron, leaving John his son and heir.

Inquisitio post mortem of REGINALD GREY.

1 Edw. II.

"An Inquisition taken before the Escheator of the
Lord the King, on Monday, on the morrow of the close
of Easter, in the first year of the reign of King Edward,
son of King Edward the First, at Purtepole, concerning
the lands and tenements of which Reginald le Grey was
seised on the day on which he died in his demesne as of
fee, in the county of Middlesex, by the oath of Thomas
de Meldebourne (and others), who say upon their oath,
that the said Reginald le Grey was seised at Portpool,
on the day on which he died, of a certain messuage, with
gardens, and with one dove-house, which are worth by
the year beyond reprises ten shillings; also they say,
that there are there thirty acres of arable land, which are
worth by the year twenty shillings, price the acre eight-
pence; also they say, that there is there of assize-rent
22s., payable at two terms of the year—namely, at the
feast of St. Michael, 11s., and at the feast of the Annunciation of the Blessed Mary, 11s.; also they say, that
there is there a certain windmill, which is worth by the
year 20s.; also they say, that the said Reginald le Grey
held all the aforesaid lands and tenements of the Dean
and Chapter of St. Paul, London, in chief, by the
service of 42s. 2d., payable at two terms of the year,

namely, &c., and suit of court, from three weeks to three weeks; also they say, that John le Grey is his next heir, and is of the age of thirty years and more."

In witness, &c.

To enable this John de Grey to alienate some part of the property in mortmain, the Crown, at his instance, issued a writ of *ad quod damnum,* and the return to such writ, after stating that it was not to the damage of the King or any others, states, that the property is " holden of *Robert de Chiggewell,* by the service of rendering to the same Robert, *one rose* yearly; and the same Robert holds the said tenements, together with other tenements, of the Dean and Chapter of St. Paul, London, and the aforesaid Dean and Chapter, hold the same of the Lord the King, in pure and perpetual alms." [a]

John de Grey died in the seventeenth year of Edward II. (1324), and was succeeded by his son Henry, who died in the sixteenth year of Edward III. (1343), leaving a son and heir Reginald.

This Reginald de Grey de Wilton, as appears by the Inquisition taken after his death, 44 Edward III.

---

[a] Pat. 8 Edw. II.

(1370), died seized of the Manor, called for the first time an Inn, " Hospitium in Pourtepole," which he is stated to have *leased out*.

Inquisitio post mortem of REGINALD GREY DE WILTON.

44 Edw. III.

HOLBOURNE.—GREYE.

" AN inquisition taken at Holbourne, in the county of Middlesex, before John de Busshoppeston, the Escheator of the Lord the King, in the county aforesaid, on the 24th day of June, in the forty-fourth year of the reign of King Edward the Third, after the Conquest, by virtue of a certain writ of the said Lord the King, sewed to this inquisition, by the oath of Roger Leget (and others), who say, upon their oath, that Reginald de Grey of Wilton, in the writ contained, held not any lands or tenements in his demesne as of fee, nor in service, of the Lord the King in Chief, in the county aforesaid, on the day on which he died. But they say that the said Reginald held, on the day aforesaid, in the county aforesaid, a certain inn in *Portepole, near Holbourn*, with one garden, and eleven small shops, with the appurtenances, in his demesne, as of fee, together with three acres of land adjacent, of the Dean and Chapter of the church of St. Paul, London, *by fealty*, and by the service of 32*s*. 2*d*., payable at the feast of Easter and St. Michael, equally, by the year. And they say that the aforesaid inn, garden, shops, and land, with the appurtenances, are worth, by the year, in all issues, according to the true value of the same, beyond reprises and resolved rent, 100 shillings, and are *so let to farm*, payable equally at the feasts aforesaid. . . . . . ."

In witness, &c.

From Reginald the property descended to Sir Henry de Grey of Wilton, Knight, who, as is shown by the Inquisition on his death, 19 Richard II. (1395), had previously enfeoffed Roger Harecourt and several others in fee of his Manor of Portpole, in Holborn, called Gray's Inn.

Inquisitio post mortem of HENRY GRAY DE WILTON.

19 Richard II.

" AN inquisition taken at Holborn, in the county of Middlesex, on Friday, next after the feast of Saint Basil, in the nineteenth year of the reign of King Richard the Second, before John Reche, Escheator of the Lord the King, in the same county, by virtue of a

writ of the said Lord the King, to the same escheator
directed and to this inquisition sewed, by the oath of
John Bygonet -and others, who say, upon their oath,
that Henry Grey de Wilton, Knight, in the writ named,
held not any lands or tenements in the aforesaid county,
on the day on which he died, which, of the Lord the
King, or of any other, are holden, because they say that
the said Henry, by his deed, enfeoffed Roger Harecourt,
William Danbury, John de Broughton, Jun., John
Bouer, Rector of the church of Shirland, Henry Babyng-
ton, and others, whose names to the jurors aforesaid are
unknown of his manor of *Portpole*, in Holborn, called
Gray's Inn, together with all the other lands and
tenements which he had in the said county of Middlesex,
to hold to them and their heirs for ever; by virtue of
which feoffment, the aforesaid Roger John and others
were seised of the manor, lands, and tenements aforesaid,
before the death of the said Henry, and at the time of
his death, and still are; and they say that the said
manor, together with the lands and tenements aforesaid,
are holden of the Dean and Chapter of the church of St.
Paul, London, by what services they know not. And
they say, that the aforesaid manor, lands, and tenements,
are worth, by the year, in all issues beyond reprises,
according to the true value of the same 100 shillings.

And they say, that the aforesaid Henry died on Saturday, next after the feast of St. Alphage last past; and that one Richard Grey is son and next heir of the same Henry, and was of the age of three years on Wednesday next before the feast of All Saints last past."

In witness, &c.

This Henry left his son Richard his heir; who by Deed, enrolled in Chancery, 3 Henry V. (1415), confirmed the feoffment which his father had made, as will be seen from the following extract from the Close Roll 3 Henry V.

" Richard de Grey de Wilton, Knight,

to John Boneyr." . . . . . .

" Whereas Henry de Grey our Father lately enfeoffed John Boneyr, Clerk, and Robert Alfreton, together with others now deceased, in fee simple without any condition specified in deed or in feoffment, of his manors, lands, and tenements, underwritten, to wit, of his manor of Shirland and Stratton in the county of Derby." . . . . . .

. . . . . . " And also of his Manor of Portepole in the County of Middlesex with all its appurtenances called Greyes Inn de Wilton." . . . . . . " Know ye that we the aforesaid Richard Lord de Grey de Wilton have

remised released and wholly for us and our heirs have for
ever quitted claim to the aforesaid John Boneyr and
Robert Alfreton being in their full and peaceable
possession of all and singular the aforesaid manors,
lands tenements and rents and services." . . . .

The Manor of Portpool or Gray's Inn continued in
the possession of the family of the De Greys, till the 21st
year of Henry VII. (1505), when Edmund Lord Grey
of Wilton, after he had obtained livery of his lands
*as son of John, son of Reginald, son of Richard, who
died in the year* 1441, conveyed by bargain and sale,
recovery and fine, the said manor and his advowson
of the chantry of Portepole, and all his possessions
in the parish of St. Andrew, Holborn, to Hugh Denys
and Mary his wife, and their feoffees, some of whom
were members of Gray's Inn. In the "Letters and
Papers, Foreign and Domestic, of the reign of Henry
VIII.,"[a] the name Hugh Denys frequently appears
as the holder of offices under the Crown. He
possessed grants of " corrody " or allowance in the
King's gift, in the priory of Tywardreth, Cornwall;
and in the monastery of St. Edmunds Bury. He
was also keeper of the Manor and Park, Wan-

---

stede; gauger of the port of Bristol, and "verger before the King." He died 30th December, 1512.

In the 7th Henry VIII. (1516), the survivors of the feoffees mentioned above, obtained the King's Licence to alienate to the Prior and Convent of Shene, " the Manor of *Portepole*, with the appurtenances, in the County of Middlesex, and four Messuages four Gardens one Toft, eight acres of Land, and 10s. Rent, with the appurtenances in the parish of St. Andrew the Apostle, in Holborn, without the Bars of the Old Temple,[a] London, and the advowson of the Chantry to the same Manor belonging, in the county of Middlesex, which of us are holden as an escheat for that *Robert Chigwell*, of whom the Manor aforesaid and other the premises were holden, died without heir, by service fealty, and the rent of *one red rose*," &c.[b]

The family of Chigwell, and the connection of some of the members of it with the property, is involved in much obscurity, and after considerable research, no satisfactory or reliable information can be obtained.

The name of Chigwell is frequently mentioned in

[a] The old Temple is said to have occupied the place where Southampton Buildings now stand.

[b] Pat., 7 Henry VIII. pt. 3, m. 30.

the city records, in the reigns of Edward I. and II. ` Some of the family are also mentioned as having property in Holborn about this time. In Parton's Account of the possessions of the Hospital of St. Giles in the Fields, there is mention of " a rent of 6s., arising from a tenement and appurtenances situate within the Bars of Holburne, between the tenement of *Richard de Chigwell without the same Bars west,* . . . . . granted by Richard de Chigwell 25 Edw. I." And in Malcolm's " Londinium Redivivum,"[a] there is an extract from one of the ancient registers of St. Paul's Cathedral, relating to the rental of the prebend of Holborn about 1322, in which the tenement of " *Robert de Chykwell,*" " *near the gate of the Bars,*" is also mentioned. And in the list of prebendaries of St. Paul's Cathedral given in Dugdale, the name of *Robert de Chigwell* occurs as prebendary of Reculverland in 1336.

It appears in the extracts from the accounts of the Stewards of Gray's Inn [b] for the years 1518, 1520, and 1524, that the Society of Gray's Inn paid a rent of £6 13s. 4d., to the monastery of Shene. In these years the Steward accounts

---

a Vol. iii., p. 21. b Harleian MS., No. 1912.

thus:—"Paid to the Prior of Sheene for half a year's rent due for Gray's Inn, three pounds six shillings and eight pence."

On the dissolution of the monasteries, the monastery of Shene and all its possessions came to the Crown, and the minister's accounts for the county of Surrey, 31 Henry VIII. (1539), contain the following:—

"Lands and Possessions late pertaining to the Priory of Sheene."

"The Account of Francis Shakerly collector of rents there, from the feast of St. Michael the Archangel, in the 31st year of the reign of King Henry the Eighth, unto the same feast of St. Michael the Archangel thence next ensuing, in the 32nd year of the said King, to wit, for one whole year."

"Grees Inn in Middlesex"

"And for six pounds thirteen shillings and four pence for a Pension there."

Dugdale, who, at the time he wrote, had evidently consulted records of the Society not now in existence, states that this Manor or Inn was granted by the King unto the Society in fee farm "for by the account of the Treasurer of this Society, made 18th Nov. 32 Hen. VIII., it is evident that the said rent of £6 13s. 4d., was

C

paid to the King's use for one whole year, and so hath been ever since as may appear by the accounts of the said house."[a]

In the year 1651, an arrangement was made between the Commissioners of the Commonwealth and the Society, by which the Pension or annual payment of £6 13s. 4d., due to the Society, from, or in respect of part of the possessions of the Prior and Convent of St. Bartholomew towards the maintenance of a Chaplain, was relinquished for the purchase of the house or fee farm rent. At the Restoration that arrangement was repudiated, and the house or fee farm rent was again paid to the Crown, and the Crown subsequently sold it to Sir Philip Matthews, to whose co-heirs it subsequently descended.

The Society continued to pay the fee farm Rent of £6 13s. 4d., until the year 1733, when they purchased it from the parties deriving title, from the co-heirs of Sir Philip Matthews.

No grant from the Crown to the Society can be found, but it is suggested that the circumstances afford ample and substantial grounds for presuming one. From the dissolution of the monasteries, or very shortly

---

[a] Origines Juridiciales, p. 272.

afterwards, down to the present time, the **Society** has had continuous and undisturbed possession of the whole property. It paid the fee farm Rent of £6 13s. 4d., to the Crown until the Commonwealth, to commissioners during the time of the Commonwealth, to the Crown again from the Restoration until the last purchase of it by the Society, as just stated; and from the time of such purchase to the present time it has held, and now holds, the property discharged from any rent, or other payment.

GRAY'S INN AS AN INN OF COURT.

Though the exact date is not known when Gray's Inn became the residence of members of the profession of the law, there is evidence from which it may reasonably be inferred that it was so occupied before the year 137$\bar{0}$. In the inquisition on the death of Reginald de Grey de Wilton of that date,[a] it is stated that he died, seized of " a certain Inn in Portepole, near Holbourn," which Inn or "Hospitium" was then *let to farm* at the yearly rent of 100 shillings. It is also stated in a " Discourse or Treatise on the Third University of England," by Sir George Buck, appended to " Stow's Annals,"[b] that " an estate of this House [Gray's Inn] was taken in the reign of *Edward the Third*, by gentlemen and professors of the common law, as Master Saintlow Kniveton, a learned gentleman, and a rare antiquary, and an aunciont fellow of this colledge, affirmeth, out of his owne search and readings of antiquities concerning the House." In Gough's edition of " Camden's

---

[a] p. 10.   [b] p. 1073.

Britannia "[a] Mr. St. Lo. Kniveton is stated to be " a Derbyshire gentleman, and a good antiquary, to whose studious diligence Camden acknowledges himself much indebted."

The fact of Gray's Inn being an Inn of Court prior to the year 1370, is still further confirmed by the circumstance that the Harleian manuscript before quoted contains a list of readers of Gray's Inn, with their armorial bearings illuminated. The dates when the first fourteen of these readers filled that office are not stated, but the first reader named in the list is William de Skipwith, Justice of the Common Pleas, in 33 Edward III. (1359); the second is John Markham, Justice of the Common Pleas in 1396; the third is William Gascoigne, Chief Justice of the King's Bench in 1400. The remainder have the dates of their elevation to the Bench, ranging from 1403 to 1483.

One of these readers, Sir Thomas Billinge, Chief Justice of the King's Bench in 1464, in a letter dated July, 1454, with reference to one Ledam, says:—" I wylde sye schull do wyll, be cause ye ar a felaw in Gray's In, wer I was a felaw."[b]

The Harleian manuscript also contains a table

---

[a] Vol. i., p. 30. [b] "Paston Letters," Gairdner's edition, vol. i., p. 297.

showing the number of gentlemen admitted into the
Society each year from 1521 to 1674 ; a list of the
names of such nobility, spiritual and temporal, as have
been admitted of the Society ; a general collection
of the several Calls of Ancients from 1514 to 1674 ;
alphabetical list of the Benchers and Treasurers, &c.

The compiler of this manuscript, was Simon Segar,
grandson of Sir William Segar, King-at-arms. Several
members of the Segar family were admitted as
members of Gray's Inn. Simon Segar was admitted into
the Society in the year 1656 ; and on the 14th of June,
1667, he was appointed " Collector of all the dutys of
the House, except Commons due to the Steward."
In 1670 he was appointed third Butler, and in
1674 second Butler and Library Keeper. Subsequently several sums of money were paid him for "setting
up the readers coates of armes in the Library." None
of these armorial bearings are now to be found, but it
may be assumed that the list in the manuscript is a copy
of the collection.

The early records of the Society do not seem to
have been preserved with that care which their importance demanded. How this manuscript came into the
Harleian collection does not appear, and in the
" Catalogi Librorum Manuscriptorum Angliæ et Hiber-

niæ," published in 1697, it is stated that Francis
Bernard, M.D., had amongst his collection of manuscripts
a folio volume entitled " Ancient Orders and Consti-
tutions of the Society of Gray's Inn." This manuscript
was afterwards in the possession of Charles Bernard,
Esq., Serjeant Surgeon to Queen Anne, and was sold at
the sale of his library, March, 1710.[a] Dr. Bernard,
Chief Physician to King James II., is said to have had
the best private collection of scarce and curious books
that had been seen in England, and was a good judge
of their value. They appear to have been sold by
auction in 1698, when the catalogue is dated, and
realized by the sale the nett sum of £1600.[b]

In 4 Henry V. (1416), mention is made of the house
of the Treasurer of England in Gray's Inn :—
" To Sir John Rothenall, Knight, Keeper of the
King's Wardrobe. In money paid to him, arising
from the fifteenths and tenths, viz., by the hands of
John Feriby, receiving the money from a certain
attorney of the Lord de Talbot, dwelling in Graye's
Inn, at the house of the Treasurer of England, for the
expenses of the household of the Emperor whilst at
Eltham, By Writ, &c., £200."[c]

---

[a] A copy of the catalogue of the sale is in Dr. Williams' Library.

[b] Nichols' " Literary Anecdotes," vol. iv., p. 104.

[c] Devon's Issues of the Exchequer, p. 348.

It may be concluded, upon the evidence afforded by the above records, that although it cannot be stated precisely when the Society of Gray's Inn was first formed, there is no reason to suppose it is of less antiquity than any of the other Inns of Court. As a late writer has remarked, " the four Inns of Court stand upon a footing of equality. No precedence, priority, or superior antiquity, is conceded to, or claimed by one Inn beyond another. The zeal of individual members has sometimes ascribed to one Inn eminence or antiquity above its sister-inns ; but they are now what they were when Shirley dedicated to them his masque, the ' Triumphs of Peace '—the four equal and honourable Societies of the Inns of Court." [a]

The general daily life in the Inns of Court in olden time is described by Fortescue as of a varied and attractive character. On the working days most of the members applied themselves to the study of the law ; and on the holy days to the study of Holy Scripture. But they did not entirely neglect lighter pursuits, for they learnt to sing and to exercise themselves in all kinds of harmony, and they made provision for the exercise and consequent health of the body, for they also practised dancing and other noblemen's pastimes. They did everything in peace and amity.

[a] Pearce's " Inns of Court," p. 61.

ANCIENT CONSTITUTION OF THE SOCIETY

In ancient times the Society of Gray's Inn consisted of members divided into the following grades: Students, Inner Barristers, Utter Barristers, Ancients, Readers, and Benchers. The earliest information respecting some of these degrees is contained in a report on a Commission which appears to have been issued by Henry VIII., to inquire into the form and order of study practised in the "Houses of Court."[a] The Commissioners, Thomas Denton, Nicholas Bacon, and Robert Carey, state: "the whole company and fellowship of learners is divided and sorted into three parts and degrees, that is to say, into Benchers, or as they call them in some of the houses, Readers, Utter Barresters, and Inner Barresters. Benchers or Readers are called such as before time have openly read; and to them is chiefly committed the

---

[a] Waterhouse's "Commentary upon Fortescue's *de Laudibus Legum Angliæ*," p. 544.

government and ordering of the house, as to men meetest, both for their age, discretion, and wisdomes; and of these is one yearly chosen which is called the Treasurer, or, in some house, Pensioner, who receiveth yearly the said pension money, and of the receipt and payment of the same is yearly accountable.

"Every quarter, once or more if need shall require, the Readers and Benchers cause one of the officers to summon the whole company openly in the Hall at dinner, that such a night the Pension, or as some Houses call it the Parliament, shall be holden, which Pension, or Parliament in some houses, is nothing else but a conference and assembly of their Benchers and Utter Barristers only, and in some other of the houses, it is an assembly of Benchers, and such of the Utter Barristers and other ancient and wise men of the house, as the Benchers have elected to them before time, and these together are named the Sage Company, and meet in a place therefore appointed, and there treat of such matters as shall seem expedient for the good ordering of the house, and the reformation of such things as seem meet to be reformed. In these are the Readers both for the Lent and the Summer Vacation chosen; and also if the Treasurer of the house leave off his office, in this is a new chosen. And always at the Parliament holden after Michaelmas, two auditors appointed there, to hear, and take the Accounts before the whole Company at the Pension, and out of these Pensions all misdemeanours and offences done by any Fellow of the house, are reformed and ordered according to the discretion of certain of the most ancient of the house, which are in Commons at the time of the offence done."

" Utter Barristers are such that for their learning and continuance are called by the said Readers to plead and argue in the said house, doubtful cases and questions, which amongst them are called Motes, at certain times propounded, and brought in before the said Benchers, as Readers, *and are called Utter Barristers, for that they, when they argue the said Motes, they sit uttermost on the formes, which they call the Barr,* and this degree is the chiefest degree for learners in the house next the Benchers ; for of these be chosen and made the Readers of all the Inns of Chancery, and also of the most ancient of these is one elected yearly to read amongst them, who after his reading, is called a Bencher, or Reader.

"All the residue of learners are called Inner Barristers, which are the youngest men, that for lack of learning and continuance are not able to argue and reason in these Motes, nevertheless whensoever any of the said Motes be brought in before any of the said Benchers, then two of the said Inner Barristers sitting on the said forme with the Utter Barristers, doe for their exercises recite by heart the pleading of the same Mote Case, in *Law French*, which pleading is the declaration at large of the said Mote Case, the one of them taking the part of the plaintiff, and the other the part of the defendant."

It will be observed that this report does not mention the Ancients. From the various entries in the records of the Society, the Ancients, or as they were more frequently called "The Grand Company of Ancients," consisted of three classes, viz., Barristers called by seniority to that degree; sons of Judges who by right of inheritance were admitted Ancients; and persons of distinction, who, to use the words of Fortescue, were placed in the Inns of Court, not so much to make the Laws their study as to form their manners and to preserve them from the contagion of vice. The barristers called by seniority were bound to serve nine vacations from the time of their call in attendance upon the Reader. But sons of Judges and persons of distinction were allowed to be of the Grand Company without any change of vacations.

The office of Reader was one of considerable dignity and importance. He was expected to give great entertainments, which involved on his part a large expenditure. As soon as he was appointed to read he became a member of the Bench, but not a perfect and absolute member—that is, not duly qualified to take part in the proceedings of the governing body—until he had finished his reading.

Various orders relating to the duties of Readers appear in the records of the Society. At one time the Reader had the privilege of admitting any one into the Society. But in 1581 this privilege was taken away, and it was ordered that "every person that shall be admitted of the Society shall personally present himself at Pension and require to be admitted."

In consequence of the great expense attendant upon the office of Reader, it was often declined or evaded. When declined, by payment of a fine, the Reader was exonerated from his duties, and allowed the privileges of a Bencher as if he had read ; and in case there should be any neglect in fulfilling the office, and to prevent any neglect of duty, it was ordered that every one admitted to the Bench, that is not past his reading, do deposit 100 marks as a *caution* for their respective Readings, to be repaid when they shall have performed their several Readings.

In course of time the Readings were discontinued, and at the present day on a member being elected a

Master of the Bench, he pays a certain sum to the Society, which is still called *caution* money.

In the early records of the Society, the term "associate" to the Bench frequently occurs. The associates were allowed "to be at the Pensions to hear, but to have no voice therein."

In ancient times an introductory course of study in one of the Inns of Chancery was indispensable before admission to an Inn of Court. In 1556, the payment on admittance into this Society was twenty shillings. "Sons of Double Readers were admitted without any payment, and Sons of other Readers upon payment of half of the fine." After the young student had been admitted three years, he was called by the Reader to the bar of his Inn, that is, he became an Inner Barrister or Barrister of the Inn. The next step was that of Utter Barrister, and according to the rules of the Society, no member could be called to this degree, who had not twice "mooted" in the Hall or in some Inn of Chancery, and also "argued twice at the Skreen in the Library at times mootible." After being called, they were bound to keep three learned vacations, and to sit at the Readings. No Barrister, however, was allowed to plead at Westminster, or set his hand to any plea, unless he had been allowed five years a Barrister.

The students of the Inns of Court and Chancery were subjected to certain rules of discipline. By an Order of the Star Chamber in the 16 Henry VIII., the governing bodies of those Societies were "advised that they should not thenceforth suffer the gentlemen students among them to be out of their houses after six of the clock in the night, without very great and necessary causes, nor to weare upon them any manner of weapon." [a]

---

[a] Archælogia, vol. **xxv**, p. 380.

ANCIENT ORDERS OF THE SOCIETY.

In the 16th of Elizabeth it was ordered, that none of this Society should wear any gown or outward garment of any light colour upon penalty of expulsion. Another order was issued in the same year, for " every one of this Society to frame and reform himself for the manner of his apparel, according to the proclamation last set forth, and within the time therein limited, or else not to be accounted of this House." In the 27th of Elizabeth it was ordered, that whosoever, being a Fellow of this House, did thenceforth wear any hat in the Hall at dinner or supper time, he should forfeit, for every time of such his offending, 3s. 4d. An exception was made in the 40th of Elizabeth in the case of Mr. Yelverton, an Ancient, in consideration of his infirmity, by which he was " tolerated to wear his hat in the Hall, any order to the contrary notwithstanding;" and in the 42nd year of the same reign, an order was made that no gentlemen of this Society do come into the Hall to any meal with their hats, boots, or spurs, but with their caps, decently and orderly, upon pain, for every offence, to forfeit 3s. 4d.; and that no gentleman of this Society do go into the city or suburbs, or to walk into the *fields*, otherwise than in his gown, upon penalty of 3s. 4d. Also "That no Fellow of the Society stand with his back to the fire."

"That no Fellow of the Society make any rude noise in the hall at exercises or at meal times."

Among the other ancient orders of the Society are the following :—

30 *January*, 23 *Elizabeth*.—It was ordered, "that no laundress, nor women called victuallers hereafter shall come into any gentleman's chamber under 40 years of age."

In the 29th Elizabeth it was ordered, "that the third Butler should be at the carrying forth from the buttery, and also at the distribution of the alms, thrice by the week at *Gray's Inn Gate;* to see that due consideration be had to the poorer sort of aged and impotent persons, according, *as in former time*, he had used to do."

THE OLD BUILDINGS.

IT is supposed that the early records of the Society were destroyed by fire in 1604, and little is therefore known respecting the date or extent of the ancient buildings of the Inn, but that they were by no means commodious appears from the fact that even the ancients of the house were "necessitated" to lodge double. As an illustration of this, Dugdale gives an account of a Pension held on the 9th July, 21 Hen. VIII., when John Hales, then one of the Barons of the Exchequer, produced a letter directed to him from Sir Thomas Neville, which was to acquaint the Society that he would accept of Mr. Attorney-General (Sir Christopher Hales) to be his bedfellow in his chamber here, and that entry might be made thereof in the book of their rules; and, among the curious orders of the Society relating to this practice, the following may be mentioned:—In the 21st of Elizabeth it was ordered, that "henceforth no fellow of this house shall make choice of his bedfellow, but only the Readers, the admission of all others shall be referred to the discretion of the Treasurers."

By an Order of Pension made in the 28th of Elizabeth, it was ordered, "that it may be known if any lodge in the house who are not of the house, &c. surveyors shall be yearly chosen to search all the chambers of the house." To carry into effect this Order, six surveyors were appointed for the North Court, four for the Middle Court, and seven for the South Court.

By another Order of Pension made in January, 1646, it was ordered, "that an exact Survey of all the Chambers in the house, viz., of the situation, the tenants' names, the terms and the rent, and those to be put together in a book of survey, distinguishing them according to the several Courts and Buildings in each Court." This book of survey has not been found. By another survey, however, made in 1688, the Inn appears to be at that date still divided into three Courts, then called Holborn Court, Conny or Coney Court, and Middle Court (afterwards called Chapel Court). The two latter Courts occupied the present area of Gray's Inn Square, which was ordered to be so called on 7 June, 1793. The greater part of Coney Court was burnt in 1687, which facilitated improvements. Holborn Court, and the number of buildings mentioned in the survey, must have included Field Court, so called from its being a passage into the Red Lion Fields. This part of the Inn is now known as South Square.

In Strype's edition of Stow (1720), it is said that " the chief Courts in Gray's Inn, are Holbourn Court, Chappel Court, and Cony Court. But since the taking down the middle row of old chambers, which severed Cony Court from Chappel Court, both are laid open together; only a separation of a palisado pail running crôss, to keep the coachmen from driving their horses into Coney Court; which since the levelling and gravelling is kept very handsome. And this court being the best situate, as to an open aire, especially the west and north sides, which look into the Garden and adjacent fields, is of most esteem, and hath the best buildings. The Hall where the gentlemen of the Society dine and sup, is large and good; but the Chappel adjoining is too small; and I could wish that the Society would new build it, and to raise it on arched pillars, as Lincoln's Inn Chappel, and then there would be a good dry walk underneath in rainy weather. Besides these Courts, there is another more westward, having the Garden wall on the north side, and buildings on the west, with some part of the south. Out of this Court there is a passage, down steps, into Holbourn Court, another passage into Chappel Court, another into Fulwood's Rents, and another into the fields."

In ancient times the principal entrance to Gray's Inn was from Gray's Inn Lane, and so it is represented in Agas's map, the buildings appearing to stand some distance from Holborn. The gate in Gray's Inn Lane is called in the early records of the Society the "old gate." Stow says that it was rather a "postern than a gate," and he thus relates how the present gate leading into Holborn came to be built:—"In this present age there hath beene great cost bestowed therein, upon faire buildings; and very lately the gentlemen of this house purchased a messuage, and a curtillage, situate upon the south side of this house, and thereupon have erected a fayre gate, and a gatehouse, for a more convenient and more honourable passage into the high streete of Holbourne, whereof this house stood in much neede, for the other former gates were rather posterns than gates."

An Order of Pension in 1587, shows the first step that was taken : " Ordered, that Mr. Aunger, Mr. Stanhope, Mr. Sherrington, and Mr. Penruddock, be appointed to consider whether it be needful to have a passage from y⁰ House into Holborn, and what way may be taken for obtaining y⁰ same." On 5th February, 1593, another Order of Pension directed, " That £150 be paid to Mr. Fullwood for a parcel of ground in Holborne, for building a gate out of Gray's Inn into Holborne, provided that the gentlemen of the house will contribute such a sufficient sum to be added to the same sum of £150, as will be sufficient to finish the building of the said gate, so as the stock of the house be not any further charged towards the same." In the following year, on the 22nd of April, it was ordered, that Mr. Aunger, Mr. Fullwood, and two others, " do view the place for the new Gate, and line out the way for the same, and appoint in what order the same shall be built."

It is related in the Memoirs of Sir Samuel Romilly,[a] that during the Gordon Riots, when Gray's Inn, in which many Catholics resided, was particularly obnoxious, he was up a whole night under arms,

---

[a] Vol. i. p 139.

and stood as sentinel for several hours at the gate in Holborn. To the shop under this gateway a certain interest is attached, from its having been the place of business of Jacob Tonson, the celebrated bookseller, who removed here from Chancery Lane, in 1697.

The principal entrance to the gardens, was from Fulwood's Rents, the receiver of the said rents being evidently the Mr. Fullwood who sold the parcel of ground for the Holborn Gate. "When coffee drinking first came into vogue in London, Fulwood's Rents was a place of great resort, and taken up by coffee houses, ale houses, and houses of entertainment, by reason of its vicinity to Gray's Inn." From this, it would appear that Gray's Inn gardens were a very popular promenade.

Fulwood's Rents and Baldwin's Gardens were at one time sanctuaries, but lost that privilege in 1697.

By an Order of Pension, dated November 28, 1663, it was ordered, that " The Right Hon. Charles Earl of Warwick, in consideration of the sum of twenty pounds to be by him paid to the Treasurer of Gray's Inn, shall have for a term of forty years a piece of ground belonging to Gray's Inn, and lying in a brickwall erected

by Mrs. Allington, deceased, on the north side of her
then dwelling-house in High Holborn,—then called
Allington House, and now Warwick House, containing
seven roods . . . north towards Gray's Inn Fields."
Thirty-one years after, Warwick Court (now Gray's
Inn Place) was built on Warwick Garden. Stow
describes Warwick Court as "newly built of Warwick Garden, garnished on both sides by large and
well built *brick houses, fit only for persons of repute.*
The north end lieth open into the passage belonging
to Gray's Inn which leadeth into Red Lion Fields."

After the formation of Holborn into a continuous
street in 1600, Parton, in his Account of the Parish
of St. Giles in the Fields, p. 186, states, that a
Bowling Green was laid out, and a house of entertainment erected called "The Bowling Green
House," on the site of the present Red Lion Square,
—then called Red Lion Fields. The Red Lion
Fields are the fields referred to, as being entered
from the passage from Field Court, leading also
into Bloomsbury. In an entry in Pepys' Diary,
dated 2nd October, 1664, he thus refers to these fields:
"After church, I walked to my Lady Sandwich's,
through my Lord Southampton's new buildings in
the fields behind Gray's Inn; and, indeed, they are

a very great and noble work." And Evelyn, in his Diary, 9th February, 1665, writes, " Dined at my Lord Treasurer's, the Earle of Southampton, in Bloomsbury, where he was building a noble square or piazza, a little towne; his owne house stands too low; some noble roomes, a pretty cedar chapell, a naked garden to the north, but good aire." Mr. Foss, in his " Lives of the Judges," quotes the passage from Pepys' Diary, to show " that Gray's Inn Square was built by Lord Southampton about 1664." There is no doubt Mr. Foss is mistaken. The buildings in Bloomsbury Square, Southampton Row, &c., being those referred to by Pepys, and by Evelyn also, and not Gray's Inn Square.

Twenty years later, in another Diary by Narcissus Luttrell, occurs the following passage:—" 10th June, 1684.— Dr. Barebone, the great builder, haveing some time since bought the Red Lion Fields, near Graies Inn Walks, to build on, and having for that purpose employed several workmen to goe on with the same, the gentlemen of Graies Inn took notice of it, and thinking it an injury to them, went with a considerable body of 100 persons; upon which the workmen assaulted the gentlemen, and flung bricks at them, and the gentlemen at them again; so a sharp engagement ensued, but the

gentlemen routed them at last, and brought away one
or two of the workmen to Graies Inn; in this skirmish
one or two of the gentlemen and servants of the House
were hurt, and several of the workmen."

In the Gentleman's Magazine for 1856,[a] there is
an interesting reference to King's Road, showing
its antiquity as a king's highway. In Agas's map
of the time of Elizabeth, it appears as a way
across the fields from Holborn, and the gate
must have been where Kingsgate Street is now.
A few years since there was an Inn there with
the sign of the Gatehouse. The antiquity of the
King's Road, which connects Theobalds Road with
Gray's Inn Lane, running on the north side of the
gardens of Gray's Inn, is shown in some proceedings
before the Privy Council in the year 1684, when
Andrew Lawrence, Esq., surveyor of his Majesty's
highways, represented that his Majesty and his predecessors, time out of mind, have had a private way
"on the back side of Holbourne and Gray's Inn, and
soe through Finsbury Fields to Kingsland, for His
Majesty's passage to Newmarket.'" The Gate is
also referred to in an Order of Pension dated 6th May,

[a] Vol. xlv., p. 574.

1670, by which it was directed, "that the ground lying without the walks between the wall and the way leading from Gray's Inn Lane towards King's Gate in Holbourne bee fenced by inclosures, and the cattle and horses turned out at present, and that gravel be digged there for the use of this Society." Theobalds Road was so called because it led to Theobalds, in Hertfordshire, the favourite hunting seat of King James I.

THE CHAPEL.

THE earliest mention of the Chapel of Gray's Inn
in the records of the Society, is in the 11th of
Elizabeth, when it was ordered, " that a Pulpit be
prepared in the Chapel, and that the Partition in the
said Chapel be removed, and Stalls made, according
to the discretion of the Dean of the Chapel." Dugdale, however, gives an account of a Pension, 16th
May, 31 Henry VIII., when consideration being had
of the King's command that all the images of Thomas
à Beckett should be removed from churches and
chapels, it was ordered, that Edward Hall, then one
of the readers of the house, should take out a certain window in the Chapel, "wherein the picture of
the said archbishop was *gloriously* painted, and place
another instead thereof, in memory of our Lord pray-
ing on the Mount." The same authority states, that
on the 8th of November, 6 Edward VI., in pursu-

ance of the Act of Reformation, it was ordered,
" that the Pensioner and Steward should make sale
of certain utensils, then being in the said Chapel,
for the behoof of the Society. Which being according sold, there then remained—

" A Chales.	A Book of Service.
A Surpless.	An Aulter Cloth.
A Bible of the largest	A Table.
volume.	A Lanthorn of Glass.
A Psalter.	A Chist."

In the first year of the reign of Queen Mary
there was " a new altar set up, and ornaments for
the same provided."

It is generally supposed that the present Chapel
stands on the site of the ancient religious structure,
mentioned in the Royal Licence to John de Grey in
the year 1314, and a plan of the boundaries and
environs of St. Giles's Parish, published by Mr.
Parton in his Account of the parish of St. Giles in
the Fields, seems to support this supposition.

From various Orders of Pension made in the
year 1619, the Chapel appears to have been enlarged
in that year. In 1689 it was ordered, " that it be
referred to Mr. Treasurer to get a Bell for the
Chapel, to be new cast, and a wheel thereto to be new

made, as he finds necessary." This appears to have
been done, as is shown by the inscription on the
bell, thus:—

> " James Bartlet
>
> made mee, 1689.
>
> Samuel Buck,
>
> Treasurer."

On the 6th May, 1689, it was ordered, "that a
model be forthwith repaired by an able surveyor
for a Chapel to be new erected for this Society,
and the Treasurer and Dr. Wake be desired to promote the said building by obtaining contributions for
the same." Nothing, however, appears to have been
done, for by an Order of Pension, made the 10th,
February, 1698, it was ordered " that the Chapel
being much in decay and very ruinous, be forthwith
taken down, so far as shall be thought fit, and that
it be referred to Sir Wm. Williams, Mr. Barrett,
Dean of the Chapel; Mr. Buck, Mr. South, Mr.
Pidgeon, Mr. Cooke, Mr. Treasurer, Mr. Carter . . .
. . . or any three of them, to take to their assist-
ance such surveyors as they shall think fit, and to
repair, alter model of said Chapel, in the best manner they can. And in order thereunto, Mr. Treasurer
is desired to furnish, out of the money received of

the Lady Allibone's fine, such sum and sums as the said referees, or any three of them, shall, from time to time, until next term, for the carrying on the said work. And that the said referees are desired to agree by the square, or otherwise by the groat, for the performance of the said work."

By a Royal Licence dated in the 8th of Edward II. (1314), John, the son of Reginald de Grey, was authorized to convey thirty acres of land, two acres of meadow, and ten shillings rent, with the appurtenances in Kentish Town, and in the parish of St. Andrew's, Holborn, without the bars of the Old Temple, London, to the Prior and Convent of St. Bartholomew's, in Smithfield, and to their successors, to provide a chaplain to perform divine service daily in the chapel of his manor of " Purtepole " for the soul of the said John, and the souls of his ancestors for ever.

The Prior and Convent of St. Bartholomew, however, in lieu of providing a Chaplain for the service of the Chapel, appear to have paid to the Society, annually, the sum of £7 13s. 4d.; for, in the Valor Ecclesiasticus, 26 Henry VIII., there is an account of the Reprizes or Rents paid out of the monastery of St. Bartholomew, thus:—

"To the Master and Fellows of
Gray's Inn for the salary of the Chaplain celebrating divine service within
the Chapel there with twenty shillings
paid yearly to the aforesaid Master
and Fellows.

} £7 13 4.

On the dissolution of the monasteries, when the
revenues of the priory came to the Crown, a decree
was made by the Court of Augmentation, dated 10
November, 33 Henry VIII., as follows:—

"For as much as it is duely proved, before the
Chancellor and counsell of the Court of Augmentations of the revenues of our Sovereign Lord the
King's Crowne, that the pryor and convent of the late
monastery of Seynt Barthilmewe, in Smythfeld, besydes
London, now dissolved, and their predecessors, at their
proper costys and chargys, *tyme oute of mynde*, before
the dissolution of the same late monastery did fynde, and
of right ought to fynde, one chappelyn, to singe and sey
masse and other dyvyne service every day yerely, at and
in the chappell at Grey's Inne, besyddes Holborn, nygh
London, for the studients, gentylmen, and fellowes of
the same house of Grey's Innc : And that the said late
prior and his predecessors were yerely charged with the

pension of sevyn pounds thirtene shillings and **fourepence,** for the salarye or stypende of the seyd chappylayn, going **owte of the lands** and possessions **of the** said late monastery : It is therefore ordered **and decreed, by** the said Chancellor **and** counsell, **in the terme of** Seynt Michaell, **that is to say, the tenth day of Novembre, in** the three and **thirtie** yere **of our seid Sovereign Lord** Kynge Henry the Eight, that the treasarur and fellowes **of the seyd** house of Grey's Inne, in recompence **of the** said **stypend of** *sevyn pounds thirtene shillings and fourpence,* **shall have yerely of the** King's highness, **for** the fyndynge of the seyd chappelayn, **duringe the King's** pleasure, the some **of** *sixe pounds thirtene shillings* **and** *fourepence* styrling yerely, **to be paid by the hands of the** tresaurer of the seyd Court of Augmentations, 'for **the** tyme being, **of** such the King's treasure, of the revenues **of the said** Augmentations, as **shall** happyn to remayn in his hands, and to be yerely paid **to** the treasurere of **the seyd** house of Grey's **Inne, for the tyme beynge, at the** feasts of the **Natyvytie** of our Lord **God—the** Annunciation of **our** blessed **Lady the** Vyrgyn—the Natyvytie **of Seynt John Baptist,** and **Seynt** Michaell **the Archaungell,** by evyn **portions."**

By the arrangement **between the** Commissioners of the Commonwealth **and the Society, in the** year 1651,

E

this payment ceased, and although the rent of £6 13s. 4d., was again claimed by the Crown after the Restoration, the salary of the Chaplain does not appear to have been revived.

The Chaplain of Gray's Inn is mentioned in the Year Books as early as 2 Henry IV.(1400), in an action of battery brought by him.

The earliest entry in the remaining records of the Society, relating to the Minister or Preacher, is in the 16th of Elizabeth (1574), when by an Order of Pension of that date, it was ordered, " that the Minister be allowed £4 a year." There is no doubt the Minister here referred to was Mr. William Cherke or Charke, Sizar of Peter House, Cambridge, in 1560, and Fellow in 1566, who is said to have been appointed Preacher of Gray's Inn, April, 1574.

In the 18th of Elizabeth, it was ordered, "that Mr. Cherke shall continue still in this house as Preacher of the same, and shall have his former allowance for the same, if it be not misliked by the Privy Council, or the Archbishop of Canterbury, or the Bishop of London." In 1581, Mr. Charke was appointed Preacher of Lincoln's Inn.

The next appointment was that of Dr. Crooke, Sizar of Trinity College, Cambridge, 1560, and Fellow in 1563.

The following letter from Lord Burghley recommending
Dr. Crooke appears in the records of the Society :—

" After my herty Commendacons whereas I am geven
to understand that ye are in mynde and purpose to make
provision of some meete and suffycient Preacher to be
conversant and resident in your societie. As I cannot
but well lyke of this your generall intention, so I must
admonish you that the good choise of the man is that
which will commend all the rest for your better devotion
therein. I am likewise informed that the Bishop of
London, whose approbacon you are principally to
support, doth concurie in goode oppynon of one who,
amongst others, is named unto you so far forthe as
he hath solicited unto him the acceptance of the charge.
The man is called Mr. Crooke, and hath taken degree
of Doctor and is otherwise, as I here, qualyfyed with
partes of gravitie and discretion such as, besides the
common duties of a Minister, are peculiarlie requisite for
that place. I have thought good therefore, for the
especial regarde which I have of the good government
of your house, as one of the seminaries of the nobilitie
and gentlemen of this realme, and as the place where
myself came forthe unto service, to recommende unto
you both the pursuit of your owne goode meaninge in
such due order of providing as to your discretion and

professyon cannot be unknown, and the consideration of this man for the fulfilling of your intention and supplying of your want, and withal the condĩtons of his enterteynment that he may be answerable to his qualitie and condĩton. And thus I bidd you hertelie farewell. At the Court, the XXX of Januarie, 1580.

Your loving friend and also fellow of your Company"

"BURGHLEY."

The next Preacher was Roger Fenton, D.D., who was succeeded by Richard Sibbes, D.D., the author of the "Bruised Reed," which is said to have led to the conversion of Richard Baxter.

Among the other eminent divines who have been Preachers of Gray's Inn are to be found the names of William Wake, D.D., Archbishop of Canterbury, 1716.

Robert Moss, D.D., Dean of Ely, 1713.

Walker King, D.D., Bishop of Rochester, 1809.

George Shepherd, D.D., appointed Preacher 12 November, 1817.

Dr. Shepherd held the office of Preacher 33 years, and was succeeded by Archdeacon James Augustus Hessey, Probationary Fellow of St. John's College, Oxford, 1832; Fellow, 1835; 1st Class in Litt.

Humanior : at B.A., 1836; Vicar of Helidon, North-
amptonshire, 1839, which, however, he resigned in the
same year; College Logic Lecturer, 1839-1842; Public
Examiner in the University, 1842-1844; Head Master
of Merchant Taylor's School, 1845 to 1870; Select
Preacher in the University of Oxford, 1849; Preacher
of Gray's Inn, 1860; Bampton Lecturer, 1860; Hon.
Prebendary of St. Paul's, 1860; Grinfield Lecturer in
the Septuagint in the University of Oxford (for two
years), June, 1865; reappointed Grinfield Lecturer
(for two years), June, 1865; reappointed Grinfield
Lecturer (for two years), June, 1867; Examining
Chaplain to the Bishop of London, 1870; Boyle
Lecturer, 1871-1873; Classical Examiner for Indian
Civil Service, 1872; Archdeacon of Middlesex, 1875.

By an order of Pension of the 15th November, 1598,
it was ordered, "that the Reader in Divinity to be
chosen shall be a man unmarried, and having no
ecclesiastical living other than a prebend without care
of souls, nor Readership in any other place, and that
he shall keep the same place during his continuance
unmarried, and not being preferred to any ecclesiastical
living or other Readership, and no longer."

This order corresponds with a usage formerly
existing respecting the vergers of St. Paul's Cathe-

dral, who were required by one of the Cathedral
statutes to be in a state of celibacy, or to relinquish
their wives or their office. According to Dean Mil-
man, the statute says "that because having a wife is
a troublesome and disturbing affair, and husbands are
apt to study the wishes of their wives or their mis-
tresses, and no man can serve two masters, the
vergers are to be either bachelors or to give up
their wives." [a]

The east window of the chapel contains the arms of
William Juxon, Gilbert Sheldon, and William Wake,
Archbishops of Canterbury, of George Morley, Bishop
of Winchester, of Nathaniel Crewe, Bishop of Durham,
and Walker King, Bishop of Rochester.

In 1862, the late Samuel Turner, Esq., one of the
Masters of the Bench, and Dean of the Chapel,
presented the Society with three handsome windows
representing (1.) Christ in the Temple in the midst of
the Doctors ; (2.) Christ in the act of delivering the
Sermon on the Mount ; (3.) the Ascension of Christ.

In the centre opening of the first window, is the
youthful figure of our Lord seated, engaged in
answering the various questions put to Him by the

---

[a] " Annals of St. Paul's Cathedral," p. 142 (n.)

surrounding Doctors of the Law, who occupy the
foreground and two side openings. Mary and Joseph
seeking their son, are introduced in the background,
while the accessories of scrolls, tablets, &c., giving
good opportunity for colour, and making the general
effect very harmonious. Surmounting each opening in
this window, and on the same principle in the other two
windows, is a light canopy of perpendicular form,
executed in various tints of white, golden yellow, and
warm sepia tints of brown, on a deep ruby-coloured
ground. This frames the upper part of each window,
and serves to throw out well the rich blue which
forms the general ground of the upper part of each
subject. The bottom of this window is arranged in
arcaded bases with flowers in each arcade.

The arrangement of the canopy work in the second
window is similar to that of the other window, but
the base of this window is different. This base
appears as a shield with label supported by handsome
coloured foliage on a ruby ground. The subject itself
shows in the centre our Lord seated beneath a palm
tree on the Mount, clothed in ruby and white. At His
feet, running through the three openings, are the
listening multitude in various attitudes of attention,
and in the side openings, a little lower than our Lord

are groups of the Apostles standing in the background, which is composed of trees and open country, and which, by the coolness of its colour, forms a good foil for the rich dresses and colour-grouping of the figures. The foreground-grass, amidst which grows the typical lily, as when He said, addressing it, "Behold the lily," &c., also affords, by its quiet colour, a good contrast.

In the third window is shown, as in the other windows, the arrangement of canopy and base; this latter, as in the first window, is arcaded. The subject in the centre opening shows the figure of our Lord ascending in glory, on either hand of whom, in the side openings, are angels clothed in white, who, with hands pointing to the Saviour, seem to call the attention of the Apostles below in the words "Ye men of Galilee," &c. The Apostles, in expressive attitudes of devotion and emotion, stand and kneel, gazing upwards. The attitudes of the angels are very expressive, and there is an absence of anything like weakness in the upper part of the subject, which is, as a rule, rather noticeable in the Ascension on account of the mass of blue introduced in the sky.

The three windows are designed, as far as possible, to be in keeping with the prevailing character of the

architecture, which is fifteenth century Gothic work.
The colouring arrived at is a subdued richness, and
shows a great variety of tint in the arrangement of the
whole. A sound religious feeling appears throughout
the whole of the windows, and the general effect gained
by the artist, Mr. Alexander Gibbs, of 38, Bedford
Square, is good and characteristic.

THE HALL.

THERE is no evidence as to when the Hall was *first*
built; but Dugdale, quoting from records of the Society which are not now in existence, says the " *Old
Hall* " was " sciled " in the year 1551, with fifty-four
yards of wainscot, at 2s. per yard; and that four years
afterwards the Society began the " re-edifying it,"
every fellow of the House having a chamber therein
being assessed towards the charge thereof, upon penalty
of losing his chamber in case he did not pay what he
was then " taxt " at. The work was completed in the
2nd of Elizabeth, the charge amounting to £863 10s. 8d.

The Hall (seventy feet in length, thirty-five in width,
and forty-seven in height), follows the usual plan of the
great Halls of the fifteenth and sixteenth centuries. At
the eastern end is the raised dais, on which is placed
the chief table, and on the right is the bay window, a
characteristic feature of the Tudor style. At the
opposite end of the Hall a wooden screen conceals the

entrance vestibule, containing the doorways and leading to the household offices.

This screen is of very handsome design, consisting of a range of semi-circular headed archways, with Ionic columns between, richly carved with arabesque and scroll ornaments. Above this screen is the minstrel gallery, with an open and carved balustrade.

In the centre of the Hall, now occupied by the modern stove, stood formerly the ancient reredos, or brass grate for fire, with its louvre in the roof above. This is now replaced by a glazed lantern.

The Hall is lighted at its western end by a large traceried window over the minstrel gallery, and on the southern side by five mullioned and transomed windows. The northern wall, in addition to the large bay window, contains four windows similar to those on the opposite side. The space between these windows and the floor is filled by oak panelling, with the armorial bearings of such members of the society as have filled the office of treasurer.

The open timber roof is a fine example of the hammer-beam type, and is in a good state of preservation.

The building and the exterior have been much modernized, and the red brickwork coated with stucco.

which, with the low elevation of the chapel adjoining, gives an undignified effect to what is, in the interior, a fine and handsome specimen of sixteenth century architecture.

The windows of the Hall contain the arms of distinguished members of the society. The following notice of them in the year 1580, is taken from the Harleian manuscript, No. 2113, fol. 107:—" In Greys Inn hall wyndowe in glasse Junii 15, 1580. Guido Farrfax, miles, Judex Ang. supremus.ᵃ Jno. Erneleye, miles, Judex primarius de coī Banco.ᵇ Sʳ Anthonye Le Fitzherbart Justicior de coī.ᶜ Lord Riche.ᵈ Justice Staunford.ᵉ Docʳ Thomas Wilson Secretary to her Matie."ᶠ

Many of the escutcheons shown in Dugdale's " Origines Juridiciales " have entirely disappeared, and the places of others have been so changed that it is now very difficult to trace them. Among those, still in a good state of preservation, may be mentioned those of

---

ᵃ Called Serjeant from Gray's Inn in Michaelmas, 1463. Year Book, 3 Edward. IV fol. 12.

ᵇ 1519.   ᶜ 1522.

ᵈ Robert Lord Rich, whose son Robert, also a member of Gray's Inn, was created in 1618 Earl of Warwick.

ᵉ Justice of the Common Pleas in 1554.

ᶠ Succeeded Sir Thomas Smith as Secretary of State in 1577.

Sir William Gascoigne, and Sir John Markham, Chief Justices of the King's Bench in the years 1400 and 1462 respectively; that of Lord Burghley; those of Nicholas and Francis Bacon; Thomas Moyle, Reader of the Society in 1534, and Speaker of the House of Commons in 1542; Sir John Holt, Chief Justice of the King's Bench in 1689, &c., &c.

On the walls of the Hall are the portraits of King Charles I., King Charles II., and King James II.

Sir Nicholas Bacon. Presented by Henry Collingwood Selby, Esq., one of the Masters of the Bench in 1798.

Lord Bacon. Presented by John King, Esq., one of the Masters of the Bench in 1813.

Lord Coke. Presented by Thomas Davis Bayly, Esq., one of the Masters of the Bench in 1875.

Sir Christopher Yelverton, Justice of the King's Bench, 1602. Presented by the late Samuel Turner, Esq., one of the Masters of the Bench in 1841, and Dean of the Chapel in 1847.

Sir John Turton, Baron of the Exchequer, 1689. Presented by his descendant, William Turton, Esq.

Lord Raymond, Chief Justice of the King's Bench, 1725.

Sir James Eyre, Baron of the Exchequer, 1772,

Lord Chief Baron 1787. Presented by his relative, Harry Edgell, Esq., one of the Masters of the Bench, in 1837.

Sir John Hullock, Baron of the Exchequer, 1823, Bequeathed to the Society by Lady Hullock.

Stephen Gardner, Bishop of Winchester, &c., &c.

MASQUES AND REVELS.

In Gray's Inn Hall were performed many of those masques and revels which in ancient times were celebrated with so much magnificence by the Inns of Court. The first entertainment of this kind, of which there is any record, took place at Gray's Inn, in the year 1525.

Hall, in his chronicle, thus speaks of it :—

"A Plaie at Gray's Inn. This Christmas was a goodly disguising played at Gray's Inn, which was compiled by John Roo, Serjeant at the Law, twenty year past. This play was so set forth with rich and costly apparel, and with strange devices of masks and morrishes, that it was highly praised by all men, except by the Cardinal, who imagined that the play was devised of him. In a great fury he sent for Master Roo, and took from him his Coif and sent him to the Fleet, and afterwards he sent for the young gentlemen that played in the play, and highly rebuked and threatened them, and sent one of them, called Master

Moyle, of Kent, to the Fleet, but, by means of friends, Master Roo and he were delivered at last. This play sore displeased the Cardinal, and yet it was never meant for him, wherefore many wise men grudged to see him take it so to heart; and even the Cardinal said that the King was highly displeased with it, and spake nothing of himself."

Fox, in his "Acts and Monuments," writing of Simon Fish, of Gray's Inn, thus alludes to the event: "It happened the first year that this gentleman came to London to dwell, which was about the year of our Lord 1525, that there was a certain play or interlude made by one M. Roo, of the same Inn, gentleman, in which play partly was matter against the Cardinal Wolsey, and when none durst take upon them to play that part which touched the said Cardinal, this aforesaid M. Fish took upon him to do it. Whereupon great displeasure ensued against him on the Cardinal's part, insomuch as he, being pursued by the said Cardinal, the same night that this tragedy was played, was compelled of force to avoid his own house, and so fled over the sea to Tindal."

The Inns of Court which seem to have distinguished themselves most in these "Revels" were the Inner Temple and Gray's Inn, between which houses there seems anciently to have existed some kind of union, as is shown by the fact that on the great gate of the gardens of the Inner Temple appears at this day the "griffin" of Gray's Inn, whilst over the great gateway in Gray's Inn Square is carved in bold relief the " winged horse" of the Inner Temple.

This union is also celebrated by Beaumont and Fletcher in a masque entitled "The Masque of the Inner Temple and Gray's Inn," and " Gray's Inn and the Inner Temple," which was performed at White-hall in 1612; and "the strict alliance which ever was betwixt the two" houses is also mentioned in the " Epistle Dedicatory" to a curious pamphlet, bearing the title "Gesta Grayorum, or, the History of the high and mighty Prince, Henry Prince of Purpoole, etc., who reigned and died A.D. 1594."

In this pamphlet it is stated that on the 20th of December, being St. Thomas's Eve, the Prince, with all his train in order, marched from his lodging to the great Hall, and there took his place on his throne, under a rich cloth of state his counsellors and great lords were placed about him ; below the half-pace, at a table, sate his learned council and lawyers, the rest of the officers and attendants took their proper places as belonged to their condition.

F

The performance on this occasion is said to have increased the expectation of those things that were to ensue, insomuch that the common report amongst all strangers was so great, and the expectations of the proceedings so extraordinary, that besides the daily revels and such like sports, there were divers grand nights for the entertainment of strangers.

On the first of these grand nights, when the sports were especially intended for the *Templarians*, the multitude of beholders was so great that there was no convenient room for those that were actors. The *Templarians* seem to have left the Hall discontented and displeased, and the next night there was an inquiry " into the cause of these disorders." A few days afterwards, viz., on the 3rd of January, an entertainment of a superior kind was produced in the presence of the Lord Keeper, the Lords Shrewsbury, Cumberland, Northumberland, Southampton, Essex, Burleygh, &c., " with a great number of knights, ladies, and worshipful personages, all of which had convenient places and very good entertainment." [a]

The next day the Prince, accompanied by the *Ambassadors of Templaria*, and attended by eighty gentlemen

---

[a] Gesta Grayorum, p. 25. Lord Bacon is said to have assisted in the preparation of this. *See* Spedding's Life and Letters of Lord Bacon, vol. i., p. 342.

of Gray's Inn and the Temple (each of them wearing a plume on his head), dined in state with the Lord Mayor at Crosby Place. The next grand night was upon Twelfth Night, on which occasion there was a great company of lords, ladies, and knights; and at Shrovetide, the Prince and his company visited Queen Elizabeth at Greenwich. After the performance, Her Majesty "willed the Lord Chamberlain that the gentlemen should be invited on the next day, and that he should present them unto her," which was done, and Her Majesty gave them her hand to kiss, with most gracious words of commendation to them; "particularly and in general of Gray's Inn, as an house that she was much beholden unto, for that it did always study for some sports to present unto her." The same night there was fighting at "Barriers," at which the Prince behaved so valiantly and skilfully that the prize, a jewel set with seventeen diamonds and four rubies, was presented to him by the Queen.

The following order of Pension relative to the above entertainment was made on the 9th February, 37 Elizabeth :—

"At this Pension it is ordered that every Reader of this House, toward the charges of the shews and sports before her Majesty at Shrovetide last past, shall pay ten shillings, and every Ancient six shillings and eight pence, and every Utter Barrister five shillings, and every other gentleman of this Society three shillings and six pence before the end of this term."

There is a tradition in Gray's Inn that the screen under the gallery in the Hall, a most elaborate piece of carved work in oak, as well as some of the dining-tables now used in the Hall, were given to the Society by that Queen as tokens of her regard. It may also be mentioned that at dinner on the Grand Day in each term " the glorious, pious, and immortal memory of good Queen Bess " is still solemnly given in Hall.

In 1613, " The *Maske of Flowers*" was " presented by the gentlemen of Graies Inne, at the Court of Whitehall, in the Banquetting-House, upon Twelfe night, being the last of the solemnities and magnificences which were performed at the marriage of the Earle of Somerset, and the Lady Frances, Daughter of the Earl of Suffolk."

In the " Court and Times of James I."[a] there is a letter from J. Chamberlain, dated 23rd December, 1613, in which he says " Sir Francis Bacon prepares a masque to honour this marriage, which will stand him in above £2000, and although he have been

---

[a] Vol. i., p. 282.

offered some help by the House, and specially by Mr. Solicitor, Sir Henry Yelverton, who would have sent him £500, yet he would not accept it, but offers them the whole charge with the honour."

The masque was published in the following year, with a dedication " to the verie honourable Sir Francis Bacon, his Majestics Attorney General." The dedication states : " That you have graced in general the Societies of the Innes of Court, in continuing them still as third persons with the nobility and Court, in doing the King honour, and particularly Graies Inne, which as you have formerly brought to flourish both in the ancienter and younger sort, by countenancing virtue in every quality, so now you have made a notable demonstration thereof in the lighter and less serious kind." [a]

In a letter dated January 25, 1622-3, and published in " The Court and Times of James I.," it is stated :—

"The gentlemen of Grays Inn, to make an end of Christmas on Twelfth night, in the dead time of the night, shot off all the chambers [small cannon] which

---

[a] A copy of the Masque, purchased at the sale of the late Thomas Hailes Lacy, was presented to the Society in 1874, by Samuel Kydd, Esq., a Barrister of the Society.

they had borrowed from the Tower, being as many
as filled four carts. The King awakened with
this noise, started out of his bed, and cried "Treason,
Treason," and that the city was in an uproar; in such
sort as it is said, that the whole court was raised, and
almost in arms; the Earl of Arundell running to the
bedchamber, with his sword drawn, as to rescue the
King's person."

The following sketch of a ticket of admission to the
Masque at Gray's Inn, on 2nd February, 1682, is
taken from Nichols' "Progresses of Elizabeth."[a]

Gray's   Inn Hall.

Candlemas: Night at 8 of y.e Clock
A Masque.   Gipps.

Nichols states that the original plate of the above
ticket had been lent to him by Sir Thomas Gery
Cullum, Baronet, who had purchased it from the pack

of an itinerant pedlar, in which it was mixed with a parcel of old coins.

Sir Richard Gipps whose name is attached to the above ticket, was admitted a member of the Society on 5th February, 1675. His name occurs in the records sometimes rather unfavourably for his reputation as a lover of order, but he seems to have been in his element when he became Master of the Revels as on the Candlemas Day of 1682 and in the following November. This last entertainment is thus alluded to by Luttrell in his diary :—"On Saturday, the 4th instant, the revells began at Graies Inn, which is to continue every Saturday during this term and the next."[a]   "On 23rd January, Sir Richard Gipps, master of the revells at Graies Inn, attended with his revellers and comptrollers, went to Whitehall in one of his Majesty's coaches, with several noblemen's coaches and six horses, to invite the King and Queen, the Duke and Dutchesse, and the rest of the Court, to a mask at Graies Inn, on Candlemas Day ; and accordingly there was great preparation that day, diverse of the nobility and gentry in masks attended, who danced in the Hall, and afterwards were entertained with a splendid banquet."[b]

---

[a] Vol. i, p. 236.   [b] Vol. i, p. 249.

The same entertainment is also noticed in " The Loyal Protestant " of 14th November, 1682, in the following complimentary terms : " On Saturday last, at the Revels in Grays Inn were several noble personages, as The Prince of Burgundy, an Italian Marquis, &c. ; where they were entertained with variety of dances ; which, being ended, there was a rich banquet prepared for them by Sir Richard Gipps, a very worthy and ingenious gentleman, who is Master of the Revels, and has constituted a master of the ceremonies, eight revellers, and twelve comptrollers."

Evelyn thus speaks of the revels in his day :—

1st January, 1661-2, " I went to London, invited to the solemn foolerie of the Prince de la Grange at Lincoln's Inn, where came the King, Duke, &c. It began with a grand masque, and a formal pleading before the mock princes, grandees, nobles, and knights of the Sunn."

6th January, 1661-2, " This evening, according to costome, his Majesty opened the revells of that night, by throwing the dice himselfe in the privy chamber, where was a table set on purpose, and lost his 100*l.* (the year before he won 1500*l.*) The ladies also plaid very deepe. . . . . Sorry I am that such a wretched costome as play to that excesse should be countenanced in a Court which ought to be an example of virtue to the rest of the kingdom."

9th January, 1668, " Went to eee the revells at the Middle Temple, which is' also an old riotous costome, and has relation neither to virtue nor policy."

The last record of these gay scenes and masques was in 1773, on the elevation of Mr. Talbot to the woolsack. After an elegant dinner every member of each mess had a flask of claret, besides the usual allowance of port and sack. The benchers then all assembled in the great hall, and a large ring was formed round the fireplace, when the master of the revels, taking the Lord Chancellor by the right hand, he with his left took Mr. Justice Page, who, joined to the other serjeants and benchers, danced about the coal fire according to the old ceremony three times, while the ancient song, accompanied with music, was sung by one Toby Aston, dressed as a barrister.

THE LIBRARY.

LITTLE is known of the origin or early history of the Library of Gray's Inn. It is mentioned at the commencement of the existing records of the Society, viz., in 1568, when certain repairs were ordered to be done to a " Chamber by yᵉ Lyberary." According to a survey of the buildings of the Inn in 1668, the Library appears to have been at that time in a Chamber in Coney Court, now Gray's Inn Square. It appears from several Orders of Pension made in the reign of Elizabeth, between the years 1571 and 1588, that candidates for the degree of Utter Barrister had to perform, " at the Skreen in the Library," the exercises which were then prescribed. But there are no means of knowing what, or how many books the Library then contained ; although it is pretty certain, that the collection must have been small, even for those days.

During the early part of the seventeenth century,

the members of the Inn appear to have taken a very lively interest in the state of the Library, and to have added greatly to its contents by donations of books. Among the earliest of these donors were the following, viz. (in 1634) Finch, afterwards Lord Keeper, and Sir J. Banks, who was then Attorney-General, and afterwards became Chief Justice of the Common Pleas; (in 1635) Sir Rfchard Hutton, one of the Justices of the Common Pleas; Sir Edward Moseley, Attorney-General for the County Palatine of Lancaster; Godbolt one of the Readers of the Society; and Francis and Nathaniel Bacon, relatives of Lord Bacon; and (in 1636-38) Sir Dudley Digges, who was then Master of the Rolls.

By an order of Pension made in January, 1645, it was ordered, that " Mr. Ladd and Mr. Bacon, two of the Masters of the Bench, be desired to make inquiry what books, and the names, have been delivered out of the Library, and by whom and to whom such things are delivered, and the same to notify at the next Pension." By another order, of the 4th February, 1645, the first " Library-keeper " was appointed, at an annual salary of 3l. 6s. 8d. And by an Order of the 4th May, 1669, the first catalogue was ordered to be made.

The reasons for making this catalogue, as stated on

the face of the above order, were *first* :—"that divers
books in the Library" had "been embezzled;" and,
secondly, that "divers others" were "forthwith to be
brought in by Mr. Raworth, according to a former
Order." The books "to be brought in by Mr. Raworth"
seem to have consisted of about one hundred volumes;
and this large increase to the Library was occasioned as
follows. It appears, by an Order of Pension of the 8th
January, 1668, that Raworth had been called upon, to
perform the office of Reader; but that being unable to
do this, "by reason of some infirmities of his body then
upon him," he had offered, by way of fine for his delin-
quency, "the sum of 200*l.*, to be paid into the Treasury
of the Society for the use thereof." And it was thereupon ordered "that upon payment of the said sum of
200*l.*, the said Mr. Raworth" should "continue at the
Bench, and enjoy the privileges of a Bencher, and have
a voice in Pension as formerly." By a subsequent Order
of Pension, made the 28th November, 1668, it was
ordered "that 200*l.* be paid by Mr. Raworth into the
Treasury, to be disposed of, viz. : 100*l.* for books to the
Library, and the other 100*l.* towards repairs in the
walks." And, accordingly, 100*l.* of the fine thus im-
posed on Mr. Raworth appears to have been expended,
as stated above, in the purchase of about one hundred

volumes of books, which books are now in the Library, and are duly, but it would seem not quite accurately, inscribed as having been, " Ex *Dono* Roberti Raworth, 1669."

By an Order of Pension of the 6th May, 1689, the Treasurer and two Benchers were ordered to make a fresh catalogue, which was done accordingly. And it appears from this catalogue, which is still in existence, that the Library then consisted of about 320 volumes, by far the larger number of which, however, were not law books.

To remedy this, it was ordered, on the 10th February, 1719, " that Mr. Treasurer do examine the books in the Library, and do treat with booksellers for the exchange of such of them as he shall think unnecessary, for such as may be more useful to this Society." And by an Order of the 10th of February, 1725, it was referred to a Committee of the Bench, "to see what books are necessary to complete the Library as to all law books," and " to provide the Library with such as they shall see wanting, or necessary to complete the same as aforesaid, against the first Pension in the next Term."

The result of these orders seems to have been to make it necessary to provide additional accommodation for the books. And, accordingly, on the 23rd June, 1737, an

Order of Pension was passed for building the Library
in Holborn Court (now South Square), which occupied
part of the present site now covered by the present
Libraries, which were built in 1841.

The library contains a small but valuable collection
of manuscripts in twenty-four volumes, some of which
are finely illuminated. A catalogue of them, compiled
by Alfred J. Horwood, Esq., was printed in 1869.
One of the volumes, Bracton's " *De Legibus et Consuetu-
dinibus Angliæ*," a folio MS. of the end of the 13th,
or beginning of the 14th century, was presented to the
Society in the year 1635, by John Godbolt, Reader of
the Inn, in 1627. Nothing, however, is known how,
or when, the other volumes came into the possession of
the Society. They relate chiefly to theological subjects,
and are supposed to date from the 12th to the 15th
century.

In 1872, a catalogue of the books in the library,
was compiled and printed under the direction of John
A. Russell, Esq., Q.C., one of the Masters of the
Bench, and the present Master of the Library, and
a supplement containing the additions to the Library,
from March, 1872, to March, 1874, has since been
printed. The number of volumes at present in the
Library is about 13,000.

THE GARDENS.

It is believed on very good grounds that the gardens were originally laid out in the year 1597, under the direction of Lord Bacon, the then Treasurer of the Society; and there is still preserved on the north-west side of the garden a " catalpa-tree," which, tradition says, was planted by him. He evidently took great delight in these gardens, and there is an Order of Pension extant in the following terms :—

" 4 *July,* 1597. — Ordered that the summe of £7 15s. 4d. due to Mr. Bacon, for planting of elm trees in the walkes, be paid next term."

And in the following year there was an order made for the supply of more young elms, &c., the cost of which, " as appeared by Mr. Bacon's account," was £60 6s. 8d.

The following extracts from Howell's " Familiar Letters," and Pepys' " Diary," show that Gray's Inn Walks, or Gray's Inn Gardens, were at one time much resorted to as a fashionable promenade.

Howell, writing from Venice in the year 1621, to a

resident in Gray's Inn, says, "I hold your walks to be the pleasantest place about London, and that you have there the choicest society."

Pepys seems to have frequently visited Gray's Inn Gardens, as appears by his "Diary," thus:—

"4 *May*, 1662.—"When Church was done my wife and I walked to Graye's Inne, to observe fashions of the ladies, because of my wife's making some clothes."

17 *Aug.*, 1622.—"I was very well pleased with the sight of a fine lady that I have often seen walk in Gray's Inn Walks."

In Dryden's "Sir Martin Mar-all" (1668), there is the following reference to Gray's Inn Walks:—

"*Sir John Shallow.* But where did you appoint to meet him?

"*Mrs. Millisent.* In Gray's Inn Walks."

Addison, in the *Spectator*, mentions Sir Roger de Coverley walking on the terrace in Gray's Inn Gardens, "Hemming twice or thrice to himself with great vigour, for he loves to clear his pipes in good air, to make use of his own phrase, and is not a little pleased with any one who takes notice of the strength which he still exerts in his morning hems."[a]

---

[a] *Spectator*, No. 269.

In Charles Lamb's "Essays of Elia" there is an interesting description of Gray's Inn Gardens after the erection of Verulam Buildings :—

" I am ill at dates, but I think it is now better than five and twenty years ago, that walking in the gardens of Gray's Inn—they were then finer than they are now—the accursed Verulam Buildings had not encroached upon all the east side of them, cutting out delicate green crankles, and shouldering away one of two of the stately alcoves of the terrace. The survivor stands, gaping and relationless, as if it remembered its brother. They are still the best gardens of any of the Inns of Court—my beloved Temple not forgotten—have the gravest character, their aspect being altogether reverend and law breathing. Bacon has left the impress of his foot upon their gravel walks," &c.

A correspondent in the *Field* of March 11th, 1876, sends the following particulars relating to a variety of birds not usually seen in London, which, during the last ten years, he had noticed in Gray's Inn Gardens :—

" House Martin (*Hirundo urbica*).—A number of these were seen flying over the tops of the houses last autumn in a south-westerly direction. They do not frequent the neighbourhood.

" Common Cuckoo (*Cuculus canorus*).—Two young ones had been seen, possibly escaped from confinement ; but last autumn a fine adult bird remained in the gardens for nearly a fortnight.

G

" GREY FLYCATCHER (*Muscicapa grisola*).—A pair of these birds generally frequent the gardens during several days in spring and autumn, but do not remain to breed.

" HOODED OR DUN CROW (*Corvus cornix*).—A pair of these birds remained in the gardens for a few hours during a very heavy autumn gale about ten years ago ; they were on the ground during part of the time, feeding with the rooks.

" ROOK (*Corvus frugilegus*).—These birds used to frequent these gardens in considerable numbers, there being usually twenty-five or twenty-six nests every spring. Last year there were several trees cut down in March and early in April, and for a time the birds left. About six pairs returned at the latter end of April, and bred ; this year they have again been disturbed, but some six or eight pairs frequent the gardens, and will, it is hoped, remain to breed.

" JACKDAW (*Corvus monedula*).—Occasionally seen feeding with the rooks.

" STARLING (*Sturnus vulgaris*).—A constant visitant.

" FIELDFARE (*Turdus pilaris*).—Several of these birds frequented the gardens for some days during the severe winter of 1874-75.

" SONG THRUSH (*Turdus musicus*).—Only three have been seen, one ast Christmas, and the last a few days since.

" REDWING (*Turdus iliacus*).—These appeared at the same time with the fieldfares.

" ROBIN (*Erythaca rubecula*).—Only one seen, just before Christmas, 1875.

" WILLOW WREN (*Phylloscopus trochilus*).—These birds always appear at the same time as the fly-catchers, but do not remain in the gardens so long as they do.

" GREAT TITMOUSE (*Parus major*).—These birds very frequently visit the gardens during the winter.

" TOMTIT (*Parus cærulcus*).—These are often in the gardens during the winter.

" CHAFFINCH (*Fringillo cælebs*).—These birds are often seen, and are generally male birds ; some no doubt escaped from confinement, but wild birds of both sexes have also been seen.

" GOLDFINCH (*Fringilla Carduelis*).—Several have been seen of both sexes, old and young ; no doubt all had escaped from confinement.

GREY LINNET (*Linota cannabina*).—Several of these have been seen, but no doubt under the same circumstances as the goldfinch.

" LESSER REDPOLL (*Linota linaria*).—Very many of these have been seen, generally, no doubt, escaped from confinement; but during last winter a small flock of eight wild birds remained on the trees for a short time.

" GREEN LINNET (*Fringilla chloris*).—These are sometimes seen, probably escaped birds; but two or three are believed to have been wild.

" HOUSE SPARROW (*Passer domesticus*).—These, of course, are plentiful, and very tame where they find a friend who feeds them."

EMINENT MEMBERS OF GRAY'S INN.

AMONG the names of the many distinguished lawyers said to have been admitted into the Society of Gray's Inn in ancient times, is that of Sir William Gascoigne, Chief Justice of the King's Bench in 1400.

Lord Campbell, in his "Lives of the Chief Justices"[a] states, "The Middle Temple men assert that, according to certain traditions, Sir William Gascoigne belonged to them; while the Gray's Inn men rely upon the fact that his arms are to be found in a window in their Hall." But the reliance of the Gray's Inn men is not merely founded on the fact of his arms being found in such window, but upon that fact, and the additional one stated in the Harleian MS., that he was a *Reader* of Gray's Inn.

Sir Anthony Fitzherbert, Justice of the Common Pleas in the reign of Henry VIII.; Sir Nicholas Bacon, Lord Keeper during the greater part of the reign of

---

[a] Vol. i., p. 121.

Queen Elizabeth; and his son Francis, Lord Bacon, were also members of Gray's Inn. Lord Bacon was admitted on the 27th June, 18 Elizabeth, and by an Order of Pension dated 21st Nov., 19 Elizabeth, it was ordered that that all the sons of Sir Nicholas Bacon, "now admitted of the house, viz., Nicholas, Nathaniel, Edward, Anthony, and Francis, shall be of the Grand Company, and not to be bound to any vacations."

The last-named, but greatest son, Francis, Lord Bacon, was about eighteen years old when, in 1579, he began to keep terms in Gray's Inn. He occupied chambers in No. 1, Coney Court, now Gray's Inn Square. In his later days, when Attorney-General and Lord Chancellor, he had a lease of the whole building. On the first day of Trinity Term, May 7th, 1617, when he took his seat in the Court of Chancery as Lord Keeper, the procession to Westminster was formed at Gray's Inn. On his right hand rode the Lord Treasurer; on his left, the Lord Privy Seal; behind them a long procession of earls and barons, knights and gentlemen. After he had sold York House and reduced his establishment at Gorhambury, he confined himself chiefly to his lodging in Gray's Inn, where many of his essays and treatises were written. On the 19th of December, 1625, with his own hand he wrote his last will; and early in the morning of Easter Sunday, the 9th of April, 1626, he expired. In his will he wrote:—"For my burial, I desire it may be in St. Michael's Church, near St. Alban's; there was my mother buried, and it is the parish church of my mansion house at Gorhambury, and it is the only Christian church within the walls of old Verulam. For my name and memory, I leave it to men's charitable speeches, and to foreign nations, and the next ages."

Among the many other eminent lawyers who were members of Gray's Inn, besides those mentioned as Readers, are to be found the names of Sir William Yelverton, Justice of the King's Bench in 1443, Sir Christopher Yelverton, Justice of the King's Bench in 1602; his son, Sir Henry Yelverton, Justice of the Common Pleas in 1625. Sir Henry Yelverton, when Attorney-General, gave great offence by refusing to pass some illegal patents. Having introduced certain unusual clauses in the charter of the City of London, he was suspended from his office, and proceeded against in the Star Chamber. In notes of a speech, in passing sentence, Lord Bacon thus alludes to their fellowship in Gray's Inn: "Sorry for the person, being a gentleman that I lived with in Gray's Inn; served with him when I was attorney; joined with since in many services, and one that ever gave me more attributes in public than I deserved; and, besides, a man of very good parts; which with me is friendship at first sight; much more joined with so antient acquaintance." Sir John Holt, Chief Justice of the King's Bench in 1689, was also a member of Gray's Inn. The following sketch of Lord Chief Justice Holt is from the fourteenth number of the *Tatler*:—"He was a man of profound knowledge of the laws of his country, and as just an observer of them in his own person. He considered justice as a cardinal virtue, not as a trade for maintenance. Wherever he was judge he never forgot that he was also counsel. The criminal before him was always sure he stood before his country, and, in a sort, a parent of it; the prisoner knew that, though his spirit was broken with guilt and incapable of language to defend itself, all would be gathered from him which could conduce to his safety; and that his judge would wrest no law to destroy him, nor conceal any that could save him." And, coming down to later times, the names of Lord Raymond and Sir Samuel Romilly may be included.

Besides the eminent lawyers mentioned above, some of our most celebrated statesmen and distinguished prelates were members of Gray's Inn. Of the former may be mentioned Thomas Cromwell, afterwards Earl of Essex, and William Cecil, Lord Burleigh; and, of the latter, Stephen Gardiner, Bishop of Winchester; John Whitgift, William Laud, and William Juxon, Archbishops of Canterbury. Henry Cromwell, second son of the Protector, was also a member of Gray's Inn. Previous to the reign of James II., five dukes, three marquises, twenty-nine earls, and thirty-eight lords had been admitted as members of the Society. It has been well observed that the roll of admissions of the four Inns of Court form a record of names as distinguished as can be found in any University in Europe. According to a manuscript among the Burghley Papers in the Lansdowne Collection, the number of students in Gray's Inn, in 1585, far exceeded any of the other Inns of Court, thus:—

Gray's Inn,	in Term	356	Out of Term	229
Inner Temple,	,,	200	,,	80
Middle Temple,	,,	200	,,	50
Lincoln's Inn,	,,	200	,,	50

In the same collection of manuscripts, No. 109, art. 5, there is a copy of an Order of the Privy Council, directing the Benchers of Lincoln's Inn and other Inns of Court, "to prefer none who refuse conformity to the established religion." As an illustration of this order, the following testimonial of Thomas Walker's religion from Robert Dorsett, Dean of Chester, 1579, appears in the records of the Society :

"To the right Worshipfull the Readers of Grais Inne."

"Whereas, I have been requested by one Thomas Walker to give my testimony of his religion unto your worshippes. These are to certefy you that uppon good and certayne information, I am persuaded that he is zealous of the truth and hateth the Pope and all his doctrines. And as he hath been brought upp by good education in the faithe of Christe so beinge nourished by you in that truth will growe up farther into a more perfit knowledge by diligent learninge of the preachers of Godd's worde and done exercise in his service and true religion. And thus wishinge unto your Worshippes all wisdome and knowledge in the lorde our Saviour, I take my leave from Oxforde the xxi May, 1576.

"ROBERT DORSETT."

And in another manuscript of the same collection, No. 106, art. 20, there is a petition to the Privy Council as follows :—

"The humble peticon of the Students of Graye's Inne; their submission Humbly praieing y^eir enlargement."

"Most humblie shewen unto y^er LL: That whereas we Thomas Luttrell and others Studentes in Graye's Inne throughe o^r unadvised facte in desaringe Woodes Stake, have incurred yor Hono^rs heavye displeasure for wch we are more greeved than for our present Imprisonment. We therefore wth sorrowfull and submissive myndes most humblie beseache your LL: of your accustomed goodnesses to have favourable consideracon of us in this case and to measure the matter with our meaninge, wch was voide of gyvinge any cause of offence unto your Honours. And all we the said offenders wth others our Fryndes shall remayne bounden unto y^or LL: in all, by any manner of dutie and service during life and assuredlie praye to God for y^or healthes and happiness wth increase of much honor."

In May, 1667, Pepys, in his Diary, records the visit of a Mr. Howe, who told him "how the barristers and students of Graye's Inne rose in rebellion against the Benchers the other day, who outlawed them, and a great deal of do; but now they are at peace again."

In the year 1864 John Lee, Esq., LL.D., a barrister of the Society, and afterwards one of the Masters of the Bench, gave the sum of £500, to be invested so that the interest of the money might be annually awarded by the Benchers for the time being, "as a Prize for some Essay on the Laws of Justinian, or on the Common or Statute Law of our own Country."

In order to carry out the intentions of Dr. Lee the Society resolved "that the sum of £25 shall annually, in Trinity Term, be awarded as a prize to the student, being a member of the Inn, who shall have written the best essay upon the subject mentioned in the notice given by the Masters of the Bench during the preceding Trinity Term."

In 1873 Joseph Arden, Esq., another member of the Society, and now one of the Masters of the Bench, " being desirous to encourage the study of the Laws of England, and to confer a real and substantial benefit, as well as a distinction upon meritorious individuals, and to aid them in the study and practice of such Laws at the commencement of their professional career," founded three scholarships of £60 per annum each; one to be awarded every year, tenable for three years, from the scholar's call to the Bar by the Society, to be designated " The Arden English Law Scholarships in Gray's Inn, and to be conferred upon such candidate as shall exhibit in the examination to be made, the greatest proficiency in the Laws of England, or in any two or more branches or divisions thereof."

The principal qualification necessary to obtain these Scholarships, is the following :—" To have obtained Honours in the examination for Call to the Bar, or to have passed such other examination as the Trustees may from time to time require."

Contemporaneously with these scholarships, the Society founded two others, one of the annual value of £45, called " The Bacon," and the other of the annual value of £40, called " The Holt " Scholarship. These scholarships are tenable for two years, and are to be awarded to the students who shall have passed the best examination in " The History of England, Political and Constitutional."

In addition to these Prizes and Scholarships, a

special Prize of twenty guineas has been offered by the Venerable Archdeacon Hessey, Preacher of the Society, to be competed for by Students. The subjects of the Examination are to be " The First Book of Hooker's Law of Ecclesiastical Polity," and the " Three Sermons on Human Nature," by Bishop Butler.

MOOTS.

A WORD or two here as to the revival of "Moots," which formerly used to bear no inconspicuous part in the mechanism of legal education at the Inns of Court

A movement was set on foot in 1875 for the resuscitation of these ancient and useful exercises; and the proposal was enthusiastically received by the students and barristers, and as warmly embraced and aided by the Masters of the Bench.

Gray's Inn was particularly conspicuous of old for these exercises, which Stow calls "boltas," "mootes," and "putting of cases." In 12 Elizabeth, Moots were ordered to be kept three days in every week in Hilary, Easter, and Midsummer Term; and in 16 Elizabeth, "Bolts" were enjoined to be held in every term on non-moot days.

"Bolting" was defined to be "conversational

arguments upon cases and questions put to him (*i.e.* the student), by a bencher and two barristers sitting as his judges *in private.*" On becoming an expert "Bolter," the student was admitted to the "Mootings," where questions were debated by the students before the Benchers of the Society. "The subject of the Mootings," says Mr. Macqueen,[a] "were feigned cases thrown into the form of pleadings, which were generally opened by a student, and followed up by an utter barrister. . . . . . The avowed object of these exercitations was, *to promote the faculty of ready speaking.* To secure this end, *the disputants were kept in ignorance of the topic until called upon to discuss it.* The case drawn up by the Reader was laid upon the salt-cellar before meals; and none were to look into it upon pain of expulsion from the Society."

As a curious relic of the times, it may be mentioned, that in 1631, in connection with these disputations, the Butler was ordered "to be set in ye stocks about noon for putting Mr. Frowle up to Moot in his wrong"—whatever that may mean.

"About the end of the seventeenth century," says Lord Campbell in the Report of the Select Committee

---

[a] Lecture on the Early History, &c., of the Inns of Court, 1851.

on Legal Education, "the Mootings fell into disuse, or were continued merely as matters of form, but long before then the system had been declining, and Lord Bacon has lamented that there was not a better system of education."

The Moots are held fortnightly during the Educational Term, and are open to all members of the Inns of Court.

The discussions are strictly legal, and by way of still further familiarizing the student with the practice of his profession, the proceedings are conducted as nearly as possible like those of the Courts themselves. The President receives the same respect, title, and authority as a Judge of the Supreme Court. The moot question is propounded by the President for the time being, and after the case has been argued for and against—generally by three speakers on each side—the arguments are reviewed, and judgment delivered.

ARMORIAL BEARINGS.

The Harleian manuscript gives the following description of the armorial bearings of Gray's Inn. " The hono^{ble} colledge of Grayes-Inne doth beare for their Coat Azure an Indian Griffon proper Sergreant wth ye laudable inscription invironing the same: *Integra lex Æqui custos rectique magistra non habet affectus sed causas jure gubernat.*"

In the Appendix to Stow's Chronicle[a] it is stated: " For armes this House or Colledge might (by the auncient custome of honorable favour usually in- dulged in these behalfes) beare the armes of the Lord Gray, the auncient possessor, or inhabitant of this House, but differenced with a border argent, and azure counter-charged, or such like convenient dif- ference. But the gentlemen of Grayes-Inne have not long since chosen for device, or ensigne of their House, a Griffon, or, in a field sables, and so they are furnished already very well."

[a] p. 1073.

www.ingramcontent.com/pod-product-compliance
Lightning Source LLC
Chambersburg PA
CBHW030838300326
41935CB00037B/611